HISTO
OF
A SIX WEEK
THROU
A PART OF FRANCE, SWITZERLAND, GERMANY, AND
HOLLAND:

WITH LETTERS
DESCRIPTIVE OF
A SAIL ROUND THE LAKE OF GENEVA, AND OF THE
GLACIERS OF CHAMOUNI.

LONDON:
PUBLISHED BY T. HOOKHAM, JUN.
OLD BOND STREET;
AND C. AND J. OLLIER,
WELBECK STREET.
1817.
Reynell, Printer, 45, Broad-street,
Golden-square.

PREFACE.

Nothing can be more unpresuming than this little volume. It contains the account of some desultory visits by a party of young people to scenes which are now so familiar to our countrymen, that few facts relating to them can be expected to have escaped the many more experienced and exact observers, who have sent their journals to the press. In fact, they have done little else than arrange the few materials which an imperfect journal, and two or three letters to their friends in England afforded. They regret, since their little History is to be offered to the public, that these materials were not more copious and complete. This is a just topic of censure to those who are less inclined to be amused than to condemn. Those whose youth has been past as theirs (with what success it imports not) in pursuing, like the swallow, the inconstant summer of delight and beauty which invests this visible world, will perhaps find some entertainment in following the author, with her husband and sister, on foot, through part of France and Switzerland, and in sailing with her down the castled Rhine, through scenes beautiful in themselves, but which, since she visited them, a great Poet has clothed with the freshness of a diviner nature. They will be interested to hear of one who has visited Mellerie, and Clarens, and Chillon, and Vevai—classic ground, peopled with tender and glorious imaginations of the present and the past.

They have perhaps never talked with one who has beheld in the enthusiasm of youth the glaciers, and the lakes, and the forests, and the fountains of the mighty Alps. Such will perhaps forgive the imperfections of their narrative for the sympathy which the adventures and feelings which it recounts, and a curiosity respecting scenes already rendered interesting and illustrious, may excite.

The Poem, entitled "Mont Blanc," is written by the author of the two letters from Chamouni and Vevai. It was composed under the immediate impression of the deep and powerful feelings excited by the objects which it attempts to describe; and as an undisciplined overflowing of the soul, rests its claim to approbation on an attempt to imitate the untameable wildness and inaccessible solemnity from which those feelings sprang.

HISTORY
OF
A SIX WEEKS' TOUR.

It is now nearly three years since this Journey took place, and the journal I then kept was not very copious; but I have so often talked over the incidents that befell us, and attempted to describe the scenery through which we passed, that I think few occurrences of any interest will be omitted.

We left London July 28th, 1814, on a hotter day than has been known in this climate for many years. I am not a good traveller, and this heat agreed very ill with me, till, on arriving at Dover, I was refreshed by a sea-bath. As we very much wished to cross the channel with all possible speed, we would not wait for the packet of the following day (it being then about four in the afternoon) but hiring a small boat, resolved to make the passage the same evening, the seamen promising us a voyage of two hours.

The evening was most beautiful; there was but little wind, and the sails flapped in the flagging breeze: the moon rose, and night came on, and with the night a slow, heavy swell, and a fresh breeze, which soon produced a sea so violent as to toss the boat very much. I was dreadfully seasick, and as is usually my custom when thus affected, I slept during the greater part of the night, awaking only from time to time to ask where we were, and to receive the dismal answer each time—"Not quite half way."

The wind was violent and contrary; if we could not reach Calais, the sailors proposed making for Boulogne. They promised only two hours' sail from shore, yet hour after hour passed, and we were still far distant, when the moon sunk in the red and stormy horizon, and the fast-flashing lightning became pale in the breaking day.

We were proceeding slowly against the wind, when suddenly a thunder squall struck the sail, and the waves rushed into the boat: even the sailors acknowledged that our situation was perilous; but they succeeded in reefing the sail;—the wind was now changed, and we drove before the gale directly to Calais. As we entered the harbour I awoke from a comfortless sleep, and saw the sun rise broad, red, and cloudless over the pier.

FRANCE.

Exhausted with sickness and fatigue, I walked over the sands with my companions to the hotel. I heard for the first time the confused buzz of voices speaking a different language from that to which I had been accustomed; and saw a costume very unlike that worn on the opposite side of the channel; the women with high caps and short jackets; the men with earrings; ladies walking about with high bonnets or COIFFURES lodged on the top of the head, the hair dragged up underneath, without any stray curls to decorate the temples or cheeks. There is, however, something very pleasing in the manners and appearance of the people of Calais, that prepossesses you in their favour. A national reflection might occur, that when Edward III. took Calais, he turned out the old inhabitants, and peopled it almost entirely with our own countrymen; but unfortunately the manners are not English.

We remained during that day and the greater part of the next at Calais: we had been obliged to leave our boxes the night before at the English customhouse, and it was arranged that they should go by the packet of the following day, which, detained by contrary wind, did not arrive until night. S*** and I walked among the fortifications on the outside of the town; they consisted of fields where the hay was making. The aspect of the country was rural and pleasant.

On the 30th of July, about three in the afternoon, we left Calais, in a cabriolet drawn by three horses. To persons who had never before seen any thing but a spruce English chaise and post-boy, there was something irresistibly ludicrous in our equipage. A cabriolet is shaped somewhat like a post-chaise, except that it has only two wheels, and consequently there are no doors at the sides; the front is let down to admit the passengers. The three horses were placed abreast, the tallest in the middle, who was rendered more formidable by the addition of an unintelligible article of harness, resembling a pair of wooden wings fastened to his shoulders; the harnesses were of rope; and the postillion, a queer, upright little fellow with a long pigtail, *craquèed* his whip, and clattered on, while an old forlorn shepherd with a cocked hat gazed on us as we passed.

The roads are excellent, but the heat was intense, and I suffered greatly from it. We slept at Boulogne the first night, where there was an ugly but remarkably good-tempered femme de chambre. This made us for the first time remark the difference which exists between this class of persons in France and in England. In the latter country they are prudish, and if they become in the least degree familiar they are impudent. The lower orders in France have the easiness and politeness of the most well-bred English; they treat you unaffectedly as their equal, and consequently there is no scope for insolence.

We had ordered horses to be ready during the night, but we were too fatigued to make use of them. The man insisted on being paid for the whole post. AH! MADAME, said the femme-de-chambre, *pensez-y; c'est pour de dommager les pauvres chevaux d'avoir perdues leur douce sommeil*. A joke from an English chamber-maid would have been quite another thing.

The first appearance that struck our English eyes was the want of enclosures; but the fields were flourishing with a plentiful harvest. We observed no vines on this side Paris.

The weather still continued very hot, and travelling produced a very bad effect upon my health; my companions were induced by this circumstance to hasten the journey as much as possible; and accordingly we did not rest the following night, and the next day, about two, arrived in Paris.

In this city there are no hotels where you can reside as long or as short a time as you please, and we were obliged to engage apartments at an hotel for a week. They were dear, and not very pleasant. As usual in France, the principal apartment was a bedchamber; there was another closet with a bed, and an anti-chamber, which we used as a sitting-room.

The heat of the weather was excessive, so that we were unable to walk except in the afternoon. On the first evening we walked to the gardens of the Thuilleries; they are formal, in the French fashion, the trees cut into shapes, and without grass. I think the Boulevards infinitely more pleasant. This street nearly surrounds

Paris, and is eight miles in extent; it is very wide, and planted on either side with trees. At one end is a superb cascade which refreshes the senses by its continual splashing: near this stands the gate of St. Denis, a beautiful piece of sculpture. I do not know how it may at present be disfigured by the Gothic barbarism of the conquerors of France, who were not contented with retaking the spoils of Napoleon, but with impotent malice, destroyed the monuments of their own defeat. When I saw this gate, it was in its splendour, and made you imagine that the days of Roman greatness were transported to Paris.

After remaining a week in Paris, we received a small remittance that set us free from a kind of imprisonment there which we found very irksome. But how should we proceed? After talking over and rejecting many plans, we fixed on one eccentric enough, but which, from its romance, was very pleasing to us. In England we could not have put it in execution without sustaining continual insult and impertinence: the French are far more tolerant of the vagaries of their neighbours. We resolved to walk through France; but as I was too weak for any considerable distance, and my sister could not be supposed to be able to walk as far as S*** each day, we determined to purchase an ass, to carry our portmanteau and one of us by turns.

Early, therefore, on Monday, August 8th, S*** and C*** went to the ass market, and purchased an ass, and the rest of the day, until four in the afternoon, was spent in preparations for our departure; during which, Madame L'Hôte paid us a visit, and attempted to dissuade us from our design. She represented to us that a large army had been recently disbanded, that the soldiers and officers wandered idle about the country, and that *les Dames seroient certainement enlevèes*. But we were proof against her arguments, and packing up a few necessaries, leaving the rest to go by the diligence, we departed in a fiacre from the door of the hotel, our little ass following.

We dismissed the coach at the barrier. It was dusk, and the ass seemed totally unable to bear one of us, appearing to sink under the portmanteau, although it was small and light. We were, however, merry enough, and thought the leagues short. We arrived at Charenton about ten.

Charenton is prettily situated in a valley, through which the Seine flows, winding among banks variegated with trees. On looking at this scene, C*** exclaimed, "Oh! this is beautiful enough; let us live here." This was her exclamation on every new scene, and as each surpassed the one before, she cried, "I am glad we did not stay at Charenton, but let us live here."

Finding our ass useless, we sold it [16] before we proceeded on our journey, and bought a mule, for ten Napoleons. About nine o'clock we departed. We were clad in black silk. I rode on the mule, which carried also our portmanteau; S*** and C*** followed, bringing a small basket of provisions. At about one we arrived at Gros Bois, where, under the shade of trees, we ate our bread and fruit, and drank our wine, thinking of Don Quixote and Sancho.

The country through which we passed was highly cultivated, but uninteresting; the horizon scarcely ever extended beyond the circumference of a few fields, bright and waving with the golden harvest. We met several travellers; but our mode, although novel, [17] did not appear to excite any curiosity or remark. This night we slept at Guignes, in the same room and beds in which Napoleon and some of his Generals had rested during the late war. The little old woman of the place was highly gratified in having this little story to tell, and spoke in warm praise of the Empress Josephine and Marie Louise, who had at different times passed on that road.

As we continued our route, Provins was the first place that struck us with interest. It was our stage of rest for the night; we approached it at sunset. After having gained the summit of a hill, the prospect of the town opened upon us as it lay in the valley below; [18] a rocky hill rose abruptly on one side, on the top of which stood a ruined citadel with extensive walls and towers; lower down, but beyond, was the cathedral, and the whole formed a scene for painting. After having travelled for two days through a country perfectly without interest, it was a delicious relief for the eye to dwell again on some irregularities and beauty of country. Our fare at Provins was coarse, and our beds uncomfortable, but the remembrance of this prospect made us contented and happy.

We now approached scenes that reminded us of what we had nearly forgotten, that France had lately been the country in which great and extraordinary [19] events had taken place. Nogent, a town we entered about noon the following day, had been entirely desolated by the Cossacs. Nothing could be more entire than the ruin which these barbarians had spread as they advanced; perhaps they remembered Moscow and the destruction of the Russian villages; but we were now in France, and the distress of the inhabitants, whose houses had been burned, their cattle killed, and all their wealth destroyed, has given a sting to my detestation of war, which none can feel who have not travelled through a country pillaged and wasted by this plague, which, in his pride, man inflicts upon his fellow.

We quitted the great route soon after we had left Nogent, to strike across the country to Troyes. About six in the evening we arrived at St. Aubin, a lovely village embosomed in trees; but on a nearer view we found the cottages roofless, the rafters black, and the walls dilapidated;—a few inhabitants remained. We asked for milk—they had none to give; all their cows had been taken by the Cossacs. We had still some leagues to travel that night, but we found that they were not post leagues, but the measurement of the inhabitants, and nearly double the distance. The road lay over a desert plain, and as night advanced we were often in danger of losing the track of wheels, which was our only guide. Night closed in, and we suddenly lost all trace of the road; but a few trees, indistinctly seen, seemed to indicate the position of a village. About ten we arrived at Trois Maisons, where, after a supper on milk and sour bread, we retired to rest on wretched beds: but sleep is seldom denied, except to the indolent, and after the day's fatigue, although my bed was nothing more than a sheet spread upon straw, I slept soundly until the morning was considerably advanced.

S*** had hurt his ancle so considerably the preceding evening, that he was obliged, during the whole of the following day's journey, to ride on our mule. Nothing could be more barren and wretched than the track through which we now passed; the ground was chalky and uncovered even by grass, and where there had been any attempts made towards cultivation, the straggling ears of corn discovered more plainly the barren nature of the soil. Thousands of insects, which were of the same white colour as the road, infested our path; the sky was cloudless, and the sun darted its rays upon us, reflected back by the earth, until I nearly fainted under the heat. A village appeared at a distance, cheering us with a prospect of rest. It gave us new strength to proceed; but it was a wretched place, and afforded us but little relief. It had been once large and populous, but now the houses were roofless, and the ruins that lay scattered about, the gardens covered with the white dust of the torn cottages, the black burnt beams, and squalid looks of the inhabitants, presented in every direction the melancholy aspect of devastation. One house, a *cabarêt*, alone remained; we were here offered plenty of milk, stinking bacon, sour bread, and a few vegetables, which we were to dress for ourselves.

As we prepared our dinner in a place, so filthy that the sight of it alone was sufficient to destroy our appetite, the people of the village collected around us, squalid with dirt, their countenances expressing every thing that is disgusting and brutal. They seemed indeed entirely detached from the rest of the world, and ignorant of all that was passing in it. There is much less communication between the various towns of France than in England. The use of passports may easily account for this: these people did not know that Napoleon was deposed, and when we asked why they did not rebuild their cottages, they replied, that they were afraid that the Cossacs would destroy them again upon their return. Echemine (the name of this village) is in every respect the most disgusting place I ever met with.

Two leagues beyond, on the same road, we came to the village of Pavillon, so unlike Echemine, that we might have fancied ourselves in another quarter of the globe; here every thing denoted cleanliness and hospitality; many of the cottages were destroyed, but the inhabitants were employed in repairing them. What could occasion so great a difference?

Still our road lay over this track of uncultivated country, and our eyes were fatigued by observing nothing but a white expanse of ground, where no bramble or stunted shrub adorned its barrenness. Towards evening we reached a small plantation of vines, it appeared like one of those islands of verdure that are met with in the midst of the sands of Lybia, but the grapes were not yet ripe. S*** was totally incapable of walking, and C*** and I were very tired before we arrived at Troyes.

We rested here for the night, and devoted the following day to a consideration of the manner in which we should proceed. S***'s sprain rendered our pedestrianism impossible. We accordingly sold our mule, and bought an open *voiture* that went on four wheels, for five Napoleons, and hired a man with a mule for eight more, to convey us to Neufchâtel in six days.

The suburbs of Troyes were destroyed, and the town itself dirty and uninviting. I remained at the inn writing, while S*** and C*** arranged this bargain and visited the cathedral of the town; and the next morning we departed in our *voiture* for Neufchâtel. A curious instance of French vanity occurred on leaving this town.

Our *voiturier* pointed to the plain around, and mentioned, that it had been the scene of a battle between the Russians and the French. "In which the Russians gained the victory?"—"Ah no, Madame," replied the man, "the French are never beaten." "But how was it then," we asked, "that the Russians had entered Troyes soon after?"—"Oh, after having been defeated, they took a circuitous route, and thus entered the town."

Vandeuvres is a pleasant town, at which we rested during the hours of noon. We walked in the grounds of a nobleman, laid out in the English taste, and terminated in a pretty wood; it was a scene that reminded us of our native country. As we left Vandeuvres the aspect of the country suddenly changed; abrupt hills, covered with vineyards, intermixed with trees, enclosed a narrow valley, the channel of the Aube. The view was interspersed by green meadows, groves of poplar and white willow, and spires of village churches, which the Cossacs had yet spared. Many villages, ruined by the war, occupied the most romantic spots.

In the evening we arrived at Barsur-Aube, a beautiful town, placed at the opening of the vale where the hills terminate abruptly. We climbed the highest of these, but scarce had we reached the top, when a mist descended upon every thing, and the rain began to fall: we were wet through before we could reach our inn. It was evening, and the laden clouds made the darkness almost as deep as that of midnight; but in the west an unusually brilliant and fiery redness occupied an opening in the vapours, and added to the interest of our little expedition: the cottage lights were reflected in the tranquil river, and the dark hills behind, dimly seen, resembled vast and frowning mountains.

As we quitted Bar-sur-Aube, we at the same time bade a short farewell to hills. Passing through the towns of Chaumont, Langres (which was situated on a hill, and surrounded by ancient fortifications), Champlitte, and Gray, we travelled for nearly three days through plains, where the country gently undulated, and relieved the eye from a perpetual flat, without exciting any peculiar interest. Gentle rivers, their banks ornamented by a few trees, stole through these plains, and a thousand beautiful summer insects skimmed over the streams. The third day was a day of rain, and the first that had taken place during our journey. We were soon wet through, and were glad to stop at a little inn to dry ourselves. The reception we received here was very unprepossessing, the people still kept their seats round the fire, and seemed very unwilling to make way for the dripping guests. In the afternoon, however, the weather became fine, and at about six in the evening we entered Besançon.

Hills had appeared in the distance during the whole day, and we had advanced gradually towards them, but were unprepared for the scene that broke upon us as we passed the gate of this city. On quitting the walls, the road wound underneath a high precipice; on the other side the hills rose more gradually, and the green valley [32] that intervened between them was watered by a pleasant river; before us arose an amphitheatre of hills covered with vines, but irregular and rocky. The last gate of the town was cut through the precipitous rock that arose on one side, and in that place jutted into the road.

This approach to mountain scenery filled us with delight; it was otherwise with our *voiturier*: he came from the plains of Troyes, and these hills so utterly scared him, that he in some degree lost his reason. After winding through the valley, we began to ascend the mountains which were its boundary: we left our *voiture*, and walked on, delighted with every new view that broke upon us.

[33] When we had ascended the hills for about a mile and a half, we found our *voiturier* at the door of a wretched inn, having taken the mule from the *voiture*, and obstinately determined to remain for the night at this miserable village of Mort. We could only submit, for he was deaf to all we could urge, and to our remonstrances only replied, *Je ne puis pas*.

Our beds were too uncomfortable to allow a thought of sleeping in them: we could only procure one room, and our hostess gave us to understand that our *voiturier* was to occupy the same apartment. It was of little consequence, as we had previously resolved not to enter the beds. The evening was fine, [34] and after the rain the air was perfumed by many delicious scents. We climbed to a rocky seat on the hill that overlooked the village, where we remained until sunset. The night was passed by the kitchen fire in a wretched manner, striving to catch a few moments of sleep, which were denied to us. At three in the morning we pursued our journey.

Our road led to the summit of the hills that environ Besançon. From the top of one of these we saw the whole expanse of the valley filled with a white undulating mist, which was pierced like islands by the piny mountains. The sun had just risen, and a ray of red light lay upon the waves of [35] this fluctuating vapour. To the west, opposite the sun, it seemed driven by the light against the rocks in immense masses of foaming cloud, until it became lost in the distance, mixing its tints with the fleecy sky.

Our *voiturier* insisted on remaining two hours at the village of Noè, although we were unable to procure any dinner, and wished to go on to the next stage. I have already said, that the hills scared his senses, and he had become disobliging, sullen, and stupid. While he waited we walked to the neighbouring wood: it was a fine forest, carpeted beautifully with moss, and in various places overhung by rocks, in whose crevices young pines had taken root, and spread their branches for shade to those below; the noon heat was intense, and we were glad to shelter ourselves from it in the shady retreats of this lovely forest.

On our return to the village we found, to our extreme surprise, that the *voiturier* had departed nearly an hour before, leaving word that he expected to meet us on the road. S***'s sprain rendered him incapable of much exertion; but there was no remedy, and we proceeded on foot to Maison Neuve, an AUBERGE, four miles and a half distant.

At Maison Neuve the man had left word that he should proceed to Pontalier, the frontier town of France, six leagues distant, and that if we did not arrive that night, he should the next morning leave the *voiture* at an inn, and return with the mule to Troyes. We were astonished at the impudence of this message, but the boy of the inn comforted us by saying, that by going on a horse by a cross road, where the *voiture* could not venture, he could easily overtake and intercept the *voiturier*, and accordingly we dispatched him, walking slowly after. We waited at the next inn for dinner, and in about two hours the boy returned. The man promised to wait for us at an AUBERGE two leagues further on. S***'s ancle had become very painful, but we could procure no conveyance, and as the sun was nearly setting, we were obliged to hasten on. The evening was most beautiful, and the scenery lovely enough to beguile us of our fatigue: the horned moon hung in the light of sunset, that threw a glow of unusual depth of redness over the piny mountains and the dark deep vallies they enclosed; at intervals in the woods were beautiful lawns interspersed with picturesque clumps of trees, and dark pines overshadowed our road.

In about two hours we arrived at the promised termination of our journey, but the *voiturier* was not there: after the boy had left him, he again pursued his journey towards Pontalier. We were enabled, however, to procure here a rude kind of cart, and in this manner arrived late at Pontalier, where we found our conductor, who blundered out many falsehoods for excuses; and thus ended the adventures of that day.

SWITZERLAND.

On passing the French barrier, a surprising difference may be observed between the opposite nations that inhabit either side. The Swiss cottages are much cleaner and neater, and the inhabitants exhibit the same contrast. The Swiss women wear a great deal of white linen, and their whole dress is always perfectly clean. This superior cleanliness is chiefly produced by the difference of religion: travellers in Germany remark the same contrast between the protestant and catholic towns, although they be but a few leagues separate.

The scenery of this day's journey was divine, exhibiting piny mountains, barren rocks, and spots of verdure surpassing imagination. After descending for nearly a league between lofty rocks, covered with pines, and interspersed with green glades, where the grass is short, and soft, and beautifully verdant, we arrived at the village of St. Sulpice.

The mule had latterly become very lame, and the man so disobliging, that we determined to engage a horse for the remainder of the way. Our *voiturier* had anticipated us, without in the least intimating his intention: he had determined to leave us at this village, and taken measures to that effect. The man we now engaged was a Swiss, a cottager of the better class, who was proud of his mountains and his country. Pointing to the glades that were interspersed among the woods, he informed us that they were very beautiful, and were excellent pasture; that the cows thrived there, and consequently produced excellent milk, from which the best cheese and butter in the world were made.

The mountains after St. Sulpice became loftier and more beautiful. We passed through a narrow valley between two ranges of mountains, clothed with forests, at the bottom of which flowed a river, from whose narrow bed on either side the boundaries of the vale arose precipitously. The road lay about half way up the mountain, which formed one of the sides, and we saw the overhanging rocks above us and below, enormous pines, and the river, not to be perceived but from its reflection of the light of heaven, far beneath. The mountains of this beautiful ravine are so little asunder, that in time of war with France an iron chain is thrown across it. Two leagues from Neufchâtel we saw the Alps: range after range of black mountains are seen extending one before the other, and far behind all, towering above every feature of the scene, the snowy Alps. They were an hundred miles distant, but reach so high in the heavens, that they look like those accumulated clouds of dazzling white that arrange themselves on the horizon during summer. Their immensity staggers the imagination, and so far surpasses all conception, that it requires an effort of the understanding to believe that they indeed form a part of the earth.

From this point we descended to Neufchâtel, which is situated in a narrow plain, between the mountains and its immense lake, and presents no additional aspect of peculiar interest.

We remained the following day at this town, occupied in a consideration of the step it would now be advisable for us to take. The money we had brought with us from Paris was nearly exhausted, but we obtained about £38. in silver upon discount from one of the bankers of the city, and with this we resolved to journey towards the lake of Uri, and seek in that romantic and interesting country some cottage where we might dwell in peace and solitude. Such were our dreams, which we should probably have realized, had it not been for the deficiency of that indispensable article money, which obliged us to return to England.

A Swiss, whom S*** met at the post-office, kindly interested himself in our affairs, and assisted us to hire a *voiture* to convey us to Lucerne, the principal town of the lake of that name, which is connected with the lake of Uri. The journey to this place occupied rather more than two days. The country was flat and dull, and, excepting that we now and then caught a glimpse of the divine Alps, there was nothing in it to interest us. Lucerne promised better things, and as soon as we arrived (August 23d) we hired a boat, with which we proposed to coast the lake until we should meet with some suitable habitation, or perhaps, even going to Altorf, cross Mont St. Gothard, and seek in the warm climate of the country to the south of the Alps an air more salubrious, and a temperature better fitted for the precarious state of S***'s health, than the bleak region to the north. The lake of Lucerne is encompassed on all sides by high mountains that rise abruptly from the water;—sometimes their bare fronts descend perpendicularly and cast a black shade upon the waves;—sometimes they are covered with thick wood, whose dark foliage is interspersed by the brown bare crags on which the trees have taken root. In every part where a glade shews itself in the forest it appears cultivated, and cottages peep from among the woods. The most luxuriant islands, rocky and covered with moss, and bending trees, are sprinkled over the lake. Most of these are decorated by the figure of a saint in wretched waxwork.

The direction of this lake extends at first from east to west, then turning a right angle, it lies from north to south; this latter part is distinguished in name from the other, and is called the lake of Uri. The former part is also nearly divided midway, where the jutting land almost meets, and its craggy sides cast a deep shadow on the little strait through which you pass. The summits of several of the mountains that enclose the lake to the south are covered by eternal glaciers; of one of these, opposite Brunen, they tell the story of a priest and his mistress, who, flying from persecution, inhabited a cottage at the foot of the snows. One winter night an avalanche overwhelmed them, but their plaintive voices are still heard in stormy nights, calling for succour from the peasants.

Brunen is situated on the northern side of the angle which the lake makes, forming the extremity of the lake of Lucerne. Here we rested for the night, and dismissed our boatmen. Nothing could be more magnificent than the view from this spot. The high mountains encompassed us, darkening the waters; at a distance on the shores of Uri we could perceive the chapel of Tell, and this was the village where he matured the conspiracy which was to overthrow the tyrant of his country; and indeed this lovely lake, these sublime mountains, and wild forests, seemed a fit cradle for a mind aspiring to high adventure and heroic deeds. Yet we saw no glimpse of his spirit in his present countrymen. The Swiss appeared to us then, and experience has confirmed our opinion, a people slow of comprehension and of action; but habit has made them unfit for slavery, and they would, I have little doubt, make a brave defence against any invader of their freedom.

Such were our reflections, and we remained until late in the evening on the shores of the lake conversing, enjoying the rising breeze, and contemplating with feelings of exquisite delight the divine objects that surrounded us.

The following day was spent in a consideration of our circumstances, and in contemplation of the scene around us. A furious *vent d'Italie* (south wind) tore up the lake, making immense waves, and carrying the water in a whirlwind high in the air, when it fell like heavy rain into the lake. The waves broke with a tremendous noise on the rocky shores. This conflict continued during the whole day, but it became calmer towards the evening. S*** and I walked on the banks, and sitting on a rude pier, S*** read aloud the account of the Siege of Jerusalem from Tacitus.

In the mean time we endeavoured to find an habitation, but could only procure two unfurnished rooms in an ugly big house, called the Chateau. These we hired at a guinea a month, had beds moved into them, and the next day took possession. But it was a wretched place, with no comfort or convenience. It was with difficulty that we could get any food prepared: as it was cold and rainy, we ordered a fire—they lighted an immense stove which occupied a corner of the room; it was long before it heated, and when hot, the warmth was so unwholesome, that we were obliged to throw open our windows to prevent a kind of suffocation; added to this, there was but one person in Brunen who could speak French, a barbarous kind of German being the language of this part of Switzerland. It was with difficulty, therefore, that we could get our most ordinary wants supplied.

These immediate inconveniences led us to a more serious consideration of our situation. The £28. which we possessed, was all the money that we could count upon with any certainty, until the following December. S***'s presence in London was absolutely necessary for the procuring any further supply. What were we to do? we should soon be reduced to absolute want. Thus, after balancing the various topics that offered themselves for discussion, we resolved to return to England.

Having formed this resolution, we had not a moment for delay: our little store was sensibly decreasing, and £28. could hardly appear sufficient for so long a journey. It had cost us sixty to cross France from Paris to Neufchâtel; but we now resolved on a more economical mode of travelling. Water conveyances are always the cheapest, and fortunately we were so situated, that by taking advantage of the rivers of the Reuss and Rhine, we could reach England without travelling a league on land. This was our plan; we should travel eight hundred miles, and was this possible for so small a sum? but there was no other alternative, and indeed S*** only knew how very little we had to depend upon.

We departed the next morning for the town of Lucerne. It rained violently during the first part of our voyage, but towards its conclusion the sky became clear, and the sunbeams dried and cheered us. We saw again, and for the last time, the rocky shores of this beautiful lake, its verdant isles, and snow-capt mountains.

We landed at Lucerne, and remained in that town the following night, and the next morning (August 28th) departed in the DILIGENCE PAR-EAU for Loffenburgh, a town on the Rhine, where the falls of that river prevented the [56] same vessel from proceeding any further. Our companions in this voyage were of the meanest class, smoked prodigiously, and were exceedingly disgusting. After having landed for refreshment in the middle of the day, we found, on our return to the boat, that our former seats were occupied; we took others, when the original possessors angrily, and almost with violence, insisted upon our leaving them. Their brutal rudeness to us, who did not understand their language, provoked S*** to knock one of the foremost down: he did not return the blow, but continued his vociferations until the boatmen interfered, and provided us with other seats.

[57] The Reuss is exceedingly rapid, and we descended several falls, one of more than eight feet. There is something very delicious in the sensation, when at one moment you are at the top of a fall of water, and before the second has expired you are at the bottom, still rushing on with the impulse which the descent has given. The waters of the Rhone are blue, those of the Reuss are of a deep green. I should think that there must be something in the beds of these rivers, and that the accidents of the banks and sky cannot alone cause this difference.

Sleeping at Dettingen, we arrived the next morning at Loffenburgh, where we engaged a small canoe to [58] convey us to Mumph. I give these boats this Indian appellation, as they were of the rudest construction—long, narrow, and flat-bottomed: they consisted merely of straight pieces of deal board, unpainted, and nailed together with so little care, that the water constantly poured in at the crevices, and the boat perpetually required emptying. The river was rapid, and sped swiftly, breaking as it passed on innumerable rocks just covered by the water: it was a sight of some dread to see our frail boat winding among the eddies of the rocks, which it was death to touch, and when the slightest inclination on one side would instantly have overset it.

We could not procure a boat at Mumph, and we thought ourselves lucky in meeting with a return CABRIOLET to Rheinfelden; but our good fortune was of short duration: about a league from Mumph the CABRIOLET broke down, and we were obliged to proceed on foot. Fortunately we were overtaken by some Swiss soldiers, who were discharged and returning home, who carried our box for us as far as Rheinfelden, when we were directed to proceed a league farther to a village, where boats were commonly hired. Here, although not without some difficulty, we procured a boat for Basle, and proceeded down a swift river, while evening came on, and the air was bleak and comfortless. Our voyage was, however, short, and we arrived at the place of our destination by six in the evening.

GERMANY.

Before we slept, S*** had made a bargain for a boat to carry us to Mayence, and the next morning, bidding adieu to Switzerland, we embarked in a boat laden with merchandize, but where we had no fellow-passengers to disturb our tranquillity by their vulgarity and rudeness. The wind was violently against us, but the stream, aided by a slight exertion from the rowers, carried us on; the sun shone pleasantly, S*** read aloud to us Mary Wollstonecraft's Letters from Norway, and we passed our time delightfully.

The evening was such as to find few parallels in beauty; as it approached, the banks which had hitherto been flat and uninteresting, became exceedingly beautiful. Suddenly the river grew narrow, and the boat dashed with inconceivable rapidity round the base of a rocky hill covered with pines; a ruined tower, with its desolated windows, stood on the summit of another hill that jutted into the river; beyond, the sunset was illuminating the distant mountains and clouds, casting the reflection of its rich and purple hues on the agitated river. The brilliance and contrasts of the colours on the circling whirlpools of the stream, was an appearance entirely new and most beautiful; the shades grew darker as the sun descended below the horizon, and after we had landed, as we walked to our inn round a beautiful bay, the full moon arose with divine splendour, casting its silver light on the before-purpled waves.

The following morning we pursued our journey in a slight canoe, in which every motion was accompanied with danger; but the stream had lost much of its rapidity, and was no longer impeded by rocks, the banks were low, and covered with willows. We passed Strasburgh, and the next morning it 64 was proposed to us that we should proceed in the DILIGENCE PAR-EAU, as the navigation would become dangerous for our small boat.

There were only four passengers besides ourselves, three of these were students of the Strasburgh university: Schwitz, a rather handsome, good tempered young man; Hoff, a kind of shapeless animal, with a heavy, ugly, German face; and Schneider, who was nearly an ideot, and on whom his companions were always playing a thousand tricks: the remaining passengers were a woman, and an infant.

The country was uninteresting, but we enjoyed fine weather, and slept in the boat in the open air without any 65 inconvenience. We saw on the shores few objects that called forth our attention, if I except the town of Manheim, which was strikingly neat and clean. It was situated at about a mile from the river, and the road to it was planted on each side with beautiful acacias. The last part of this voyage was performed close under land, as the wind was so violently against us, that even with all the force of a rapid current in our favour, we were hardly permitted to proceed. We were told (and not without reason) that we ought to congratulate ourselves on having exchanged our canoe for this boat, as the river was now of considerable width, and tossed by the wind into large 66 waves. The same morning a boat, containing fifteen persons, in attempting to cross the water, had upset in the middle of the river, and every one in it perished. We saw the boat turned over, floating down the stream. This was a melancholy sight, yet ludicrously commented on by the *batalier*; almost the whole stock of whose French consisted in the word *seulement*. When we asked him what had happened, he answered, laying particular emphasis on this favourite dissyllable, *C'est seulement un bateau, qui etoit seulement renversèe, et tous les peuples sont seulement noyès.*

Mayence is one of the best fortified towns in Germany. The river, which 67 is broad and rapid, guards it to the east, and the hills for three leagues around exhibit signs of fortifications. The town itself is old, the streets narrow, and the houses high: the cathedral and towers of the town still bear marks of the bombardment which took place in the revolutionary war.

We took our place in the DILIGENCE PAR-EAU for Cologne, and the next morning (September 4th) departed. This conveyance appeared much more like a mercantile English affair than any we had before seen; it was shaped like a steam-boat, with a cabin and a high deck. Most of our companions chose to remain in the cabin; this was fortunate for us, since nothing could be more horribly disgusting than the lower order of smoking, drinking Germans who travelled with us; they swaggered and talked, and what was hideous to English eyes, kissed one another: there were, however, two or three merchants of a better class, who appeared well-informed and polite.

The part of the Rhine down which we now glided, is that so beautifully described by Lord Byron in his third canto of *Childe Harold*. We read these verses with delight, as they conjured before us these lovely scenes with the truth and vividness of painting, and with the exquisite addition of glowing language and a warm imagination. We were carried down by a dangerously rapid current, and saw on either side of us hills covered with vines and trees, craggy cliffs crowned by desolate towers, and wooded islands, where picturesque ruins peeped from behind the foliage, and cast the shadows of their forms on the troubled waters, which distorted without deforming them. We heard the songs of the vintagers, and if surrounded by disgusting Germans, the sight was not so replete with enjoyment as I now fancy it to have been; yet memory, taking all the dark shades from the picture, presents this part of the Rhine to my remembrance as the loveliest paradise on earth.

We had sufficient leisure for the enjoyment of these scenes, for the boatmen, neither rowing nor steering, suffered us to be carried down by the stream, and the boat turned round and round as it descended.

While I speak with disgust of the Germans who travelled with us, I should in justice to these borderers record, that at one of the inns here we saw the only pretty woman we met with in the course of our travels. She is what I should conceive to be a truly German beauty; grey eyes, slightly tinged with brown, and expressive of uncommon sweetness and frankness. She had lately recovered from a fever, and this added to the interest of her countenance, by adorning it with an appearance of extreme delicacy.

On the following day we left the hills of the Rhine, and found that, for the remainder of our journey, we should move sluggishly through the flats of Holland: the river also winds extremely, so that, after calculating our resources, we resolved to finish our journey in a land diligence. Our water conveyance remained that night at Bonn, and that we might lose no time, we proceeded post the same night to Cologne, where we arrived late; for the rate of travelling in Germany seldom exceeds a mile and a half an hour.

Cologne appeared an immense town, as we drove through street after street to arrive at our inn. Before we slept, we secured places in the diligence, which was to depart next morning for Clêves.

Nothing in the world can be more wretched than travelling in this German diligence: the coach is clumsy and comfortless, and we proceeded so slowly, stopping so often, that it appeared as if we should never arrive at our journey's end. We were allowed two hours for dinner, and two more were wasted in the evening while the coach was being changed. We were then requested, as the diligence had a greater demand for places than it could supply, to proceed in a CABRIOLET which was provided for us. We readily consented, as we hoped to travel faster than in the heavy diligence; but this was not permitted, and we jogged on all night behind this cumbrous machine. In the morning when we stopped, and for a moment indulged a hope that we had arrived at Clêves, which was at the distance of five leagues from our last night's stage; but we had only advanced three leagues in seven or eight hours, and had yet eight miles to perform. However, we first rested about three hours at this stage, where we could not obtain breakfast or any convenience, and at about eight o'clock we again departed, and with slow, although far from easy travelling, faint with hunger and fatigue, we arrived by noon at Clêves.

HOLLAND.

Tired by the slow pace of the diligence, we resolved to post the remainder of the way. We had now, however, left Germany, and travelled at about the same rate as an English post-chaise. The country was entirely flat, and the roads so sandy, that the horses proceeded with difficulty. The only ornaments of this country are the turf fortifications that surround the towns. At Nimeguen we passed the flying bridge, mentioned in the letters of Lady Mary Montague. We had intended to travel all night, but at Triel, where we arrived at about ten o'clock, we were assured that no post-boy was to be found who would proceed at so late an hour, on account of the robbers who infested the roads. This was an obvious imposition; but as we could procure neither horses nor driver, we were obliged to sleep here.

During the whole of the following day the road lay between canals, which intersect this country in every direction. The roads were excellent, but the Dutch have contrived as many inconveniences as possible. In our journey of the day before, we had passed by a windmill, which was so situated with regard to the road, that it was only by keeping close to the opposite side, and passing quickly, that we could avoid the sweep of its sails.

The roads between the canals were only wide enough to admit of one carriage, so that when we encountered another we were obliged sometimes to back for half a mile, until we should come to one of the drawbridges which led to the fields, on which one of the CABRIOLETS was rolled, while the other passed. But they have another practice, which is still more annoying: the flax when cut is put to soak under the mud of the canals, and then placed to dry against the trees which are planted on either side of the road; the stench that it exhales, when the beams of the sun draw out the moisture, is scarcely endurable. We saw many enormous frogs and toads in the canals; and the only sight which refreshed the eye by its beauty was the delicious verdure of the fields, where the grass was as rich and green as that of England, an appearance not common on the continent.

Rotterdam is remarkably clean: the Dutch even wash the outside brickwork of their houses. We remained here one day, and met with a man in a very unfortunate condition: he had been born in Holland, and had spent so much of his life between England, France, and Germany, that he had acquired a slight knowledge of the language of each country, and spoke all very imperfectly. He said that he understood English best, but he was nearly unable to express himself in that.

On the evening of the 8th of August we sailed from Rotterdam, but contrary winds obliged us to remain nearly two days at Marsluys, a town about two leagues from Rotterdam. Here our last guinea was expended, and we reflected with wonder that we had travelled eight hundred miles for less than thirty pounds, passing through lovely scenes, and enjoying the beauteous Rhine, and all the brilliant shews of earth and sky, perhaps more, travelling as we did, in an open boat, than if we had been shut up in a carriage, and passed on the road under the hills.

The captain of our vessel was an Englishman, and had been a king's pilot. The bar of the Rhine a little below Marsluys is so dangerous, that without a very favourable breeze none of the Dutch vessels dare attempt its passage; but although the wind was a very few points in our favour, our captain resolved to sail, and although half repentant before he had accomplished his undertaking, he was glad and proud when, triumphing over the timorous Dutchmen, the bar was crossed, and the vessel safe in the open sea. It was in truth an enterprise of some peril; a heavy gale had prevailed during the night, and although it had abated since the morning, the breakers at the bar were still exceedingly high. Through some delay, which had arisen from the ship having got a-ground in the harbour, we arrived half an hour after the appointed time. The breakers were tremendous, and we were informed that there was the space of only two feet between the bottom of the vessel and the sands. The waves, which broke against the sides of the ship with a terrible shock, were quite perpendicular, and even sometimes overhanging in the abrupt smoothness of their sides. Shoals of enormous porpoises were sporting with the utmost composure amidst the troubled waters.

We safely past this danger, and after a navigation unexpectedly short, arrived at Gravesend on the morning of the 13th of September, the third day after our departure from Marsluys.

M.

LETTERS.

LETTERS

WRITTEN

DURING A RESIDENCE OF THREE MONTHS IN THE ENVIRONS OF GENEVA,

IN THE SUMMER OF THE YEAR 1816.
LETTER I.

Hôtel de Secheron, Geneva,
May 17, 1816.

We arrived at Paris on the 8th of this month, and were detained two days for the purpose of obtaining the various signatures necessary to our passports, the French government having become much more circumspect since the escape of Lavalette. We had no letters of introduction, or any friend in that city, and were therefore confined to our hotel, where we were obliged to hire apartments for the week, although when we first arrived we expected to be detained one night only; for in Paris there are no houses where you can be accommodated with apartments by the day.

The manners of the French are interesting, although less attractive, at least to Englishmen, than before the last invasion of the Allies: the discontent and sullenness of their minds perpetually betrays itself. Nor is it wonderful that they should regard the subjects of a government which fills their country with hostile garrisons, and sustains a detested dynasty on the throne, with an acrimony and indignation of which that government alone is the proper object. This feeling is honourable to the French, and encouraging to all those of every nation in Europe who have a fellow feeling with the oppressed, and who cherish an unconquerable hope that the cause of liberty must at length prevail.

Our route after Paris, as far as Troyes, lay through the same uninteresting tract of country which we had traversed on foot nearly two years before, but on quitting Troyes we left the road leading to Neufchâtel, to follow that which was to conduct us to Geneva. We entered Dijon on the third evening after our departure from Paris, and passing through Dôle, arrived at Poligny. This town is built at the foot of Jura, which rises abruptly from a plain of vast extent. The rocks of the mountain overhang the houses. Some difficulty in procuring horses detained us here until the evening closed in, when we proceeded, by the light of a stormy moon, to Champagnolles, a little village situated in the depth of the mountains. The road was serpentine and exceedingly steep, and was overhung on one side by half distinguished precipices, whilst the other was a gulph, filled by the darkness of the driving clouds. The dashing of the invisible mountain streams announced to us that we had quitted the plains of France, as we slowly ascended, amidst a violent storm of wind and rain, to Champagnolles, where we arrived at twelve o'clock, the fourth night after our departure from Paris.

The next morning we proceeded, still ascending among the ravines and vallies of the mountain. The scenery perpetually grows more wonderful and sublime: pine forests of impenetrable thickness, and untrodden, nay, inaccessible expanse spread on every side. Sometimes the dark woods descending, follow the route into the vallies, the distorted trees struggling with knotted roots between the most barren clefts; 90 sometimes the road winds high into the regions of frost, and then the forests become scattered, and the branches of the trees are loaded with snow, and half of the enormous pines themselves buried in the wavy drifts. The spring, as the inhabitants informed us, was unusually late, and indeed the cold was excessive; as we ascended the mountains, the same clouds which rained on us in the vallies poured forth large flakes of snow thick and fast. The sun occasionally shone through these showers, and illuminated the magnificent ravines of the mountains, whose gigantic pines were some laden with snow, some wreathed round by the lines of scattered and lingering vapour; others 91 darting their dark spires into the sunny sky, brilliantly clear and azure.

As the evening advanced, and we ascended higher, the snow, which we had beheld whitening the overhanging rocks, now encroached upon our road, and it snowed fast as we entered the village of Les Rousses, where we were threatened by the apparent necessity of passing the night in a bad inn and dirty beds. For from that place there are two roads to Geneva; one by Nion, in the Swiss territory, where the mountain route is shorter, and comparatively easy at that time of the year, when the road is for several leagues covered with snow of an enormous depth; the other road lay 92 through Gex, and was too circuitous and dangerous to be attempted at so late an hour in the day. Our passport, however, was for Gex, and we were told that we could not change its destination; but all these police laws, so severe in themselves, are to be softened by bribery, and this difficulty was at length overcome. We hired four horses, and ten men to support the carriage, and departed from Les Rousses at six in the evening, when the sun had already far descended, and the snow pelting against the windows of our carriage, assisted the coming darkness to deprive us of the view of the lake of Geneva and the far distant Alps.

93 The prospect around, however, was sufficiently sublime to command our attention—never was scene more awfully desolate. The trees in these regions are incredibly large, and stand in scattered clumps over the white wilderness; the vast expanse of snow was chequered only by these gigantic pines, and the poles that marked our road: no river or rock-encircled lawn relieved the eye, by adding the picturesque to the sublime. The natural

silence of that uninhabited desert contrasted strangely with the voices of the men who conducted us, who, with animated tones and gestures, called to one another in a PATOIS composed of French and Italian, creating disturbance, where but for them, there was none.

To what a different scene are we now arrived! To the warm sunshine and to the humming of sun-loving insects. From the windows of our hotel we see the lovely lake, blue as the heavens which it reflects, and sparkling with golden beams. The opposite shore is sloping, and covered with vines, which however do not so early in the season add to the beauty of the prospect. Gentlemens' seats are scattered over these banks, behind which rise the various ridges of black mountains, and towering far above, in the midst of its snowy Alps, the majestic Mont Blanc, highest and queen of all. Such is the view reflected by the lake; it is a bright summer scene without any of that sacred solitude and deep seclusion that delighted us at Lucerne.

We have not yet found out any very agreeable walks, but you know our attachment to water excursions. We have hired a boat, and every evening at about six o'clock we sail on the lake, which is delightful, whether we glide over a glassy surface or are speeded along by a strong wind. The waves of this lake never afflict me with that sickness that deprives me of all enjoyment in a sea voyage; on the contrary, the tossing of our boat raises my spirits and inspires me with unusual hilarity. Twilight here is of short duration, but we at present enjoy the benefit of an increasing moon, and seldom return until ten o'clock, when, as we approach the shore, we are saluted by the delightful scent of flowers and new mown grass, and the chirp of the grasshoppers, and the song of the evening birds.

We do not enter into society here, yet our time passes swiftly and delightfully. We read Latin and Italian during the heats of noon, and when the sun declines we walk in the garden of the hotel, looking at the rabbits, relieving fallen cockchafers, and watching the motions of a myriad of lizards, who inhabit a southern wall of the garden. You know that we have just escaped from the gloom of winter and of London; and coming to this delightful spot during this divine weather, I feel as happy as a new-fledged bird, and hardly care what twig I fly to, so that I may try my new-found wings. A more experienced bird may be more difficult in its choice of a bower; but in my present temper of mind, the budding flowers, the fresh grass of spring, and the happy creatures about me that live and enjoy these pleasures, are quite enough to afford me exquisite delight, even though clouds should shut out Mont Blanc from my sight. Adieu!

M.

LETTER II.

COLIGNY—GENEVA—PLAINPALAIS.

Campagne C******, near Coligny,
1st June.

You will perceive from my date that we have changed our residence since my last letter. We now inhabit a little cottage on the opposite shore of the lake, and have exchanged the view of Mont Blanc and her snowy AIGUILLES for the dark frowning Jura, behind whose range we every evening see the sun sink, and darkness approaches our valley from behind the Alps, which are then tinged by that glowing rose-like hue which is observed in England to attend on the clouds of an autumnal sky when daylight is almost gone. The lake is at our feet, and a little harbour contains our boat, in which we still enjoy our evening excursions on the water. Unfortunately we do not now enjoy those brilliant skies that hailed us on our first arrival to this country. An almost perpetual rain confines us principally to the house; but when the sun bursts forth it is with a splendour and heat unknown in England. The thunder storms that visit us are grander and more terrific than I have ever seen before. We watch them as they approach from the opposite side of the lake, observing the lightning play among the clouds in various parts of the heavens, and dart in jagged figures upon the piny heights of Jura, dark with the shadow of the overhanging cloud, while perhaps the sun is shining cheerily upon us. One night we ENJOYED a finer storm than I had ever before beheld. The lake was lit up—the pines on Jura made visible, and all the scene illuminated for an instant, when a pitchy blackness succeeded, and the thunder came in frightful bursts over our heads amid the darkness.

But while I still dwell on the country around Geneva, you will expect me to say something of the town itself: there is nothing, however, in it that can repay you for the trouble of walking over its rough stones. The houses are high, the streets narrow, many of them on the ascent, and no public building of any beauty to attract your eye, or any architecture to gratify your taste. The town is surrounded by a wall, the three gates of which are shut exactly at ten o'clock, when no bribery (as in France) can open them. To the south of the town is the promenade of the Genevese, a grassy plain planted with a few trees, and called Plainpalais. Here a small obelisk is erected to the glory of Rousseau, and here (such is the mutability of human life) the magistrates, the successors of those who exiled him from his native country, [102] were shot by the populace during that revolution, which his writings mainly contributed to mature, and which, notwithstanding the temporary bloodshed and injustice with which it was polluted, has produced enduring benefits to mankind, which all the chicanery of statesmen, nor even the great conspiracy of kings, can entirely render vain. From respect to the memory of their predecessors, none of the present magistrates ever walk in Plainpalais. Another Sunday recreation for the citizens is an excursion to the top of Mont Salève. This hill is within a league of the town, and rises perpendicularly from the cultivated plain. It is ascended on the other side, and I should [103] judge from its situation that your toil is rewarded by a delightful view of the course of the Rhone and Arve, and of the shores of the lake. We have not yet visited it.

There is more equality of classes here than in England. This occasions a greater freedom and refinement of manners among the lower orders than we meet with in our own country. I fancy the haughty English ladies are greatly disgusted with this consequence of republican institutions, for the Genevese servants complain very much of their SCOLDING, an exercise of the tongue, I believe, perfectly unknown here. The peasants of Switzerland may not however emulate the vivacity [104] and grace of the French. They are more cleanly, but they are slow and inapt. I know a girl of twenty, who although she had lived all her life among vineyards, could not inform me during what month the vintage took place, and I discovered she was utterly ignorant of the order in which the months succeed to one another. She would not have been surprised if I had talked of the burning sun and delicious fruits of December, or of the frosts of July. Yet she is by no means deficient in understanding.

The Genevese are also much inclined to puritanism. It is true that from habit they dance on a Sunday, but as soon as the French government was [105] abolished in the town, the magistrates ordered the theatre to be closed, and measures were taken to pull down the building.

We have latterly enjoyed fine weather, and nothing is more pleasant than to listen to the evening song of the vine-dressers. They are all women, and most of them have harmonious although masculine voices. The theme of their ballads consists of shepherds, love, flocks, and the sons of kings who fall in love with beautiful shepherdesses. Their tunes are monotonous, but it is sweet to hear them in the stillness of evening, while we are enjoying the sight of the setting sun, either from the hill behind our house or from the lake.

Such are our pleasures here, which would be greatly increased if the season had been more favourable, for they chiefly consist in such enjoyments as sunshine and gentle breezes bestow. We have not yet made any excursion in the environs of the town, but we have planned several, when you shall again hear of us; and we will endeavour, by the magic of words, to transport the ethereal part of you to the neighbourhood of the Alps, and mountain streams, and forests, which, while they clothe the former, darken the latter with their vast shadows. Adieu!

M.

LETTER III.

To T. P. Esq.

MELLTERIE—CLAREN—SCHILLON—VEVAI—LAUSANNE.

Montalegre, near Coligni, Geneva,
July 12th.

It is nearly a fortnight since I have returned from Vevai. This journey has been on every account delightful, but most especially, because then I first knew the divine beauty of Rousseau's imagination, as it exhibits itself in Julie. It is inconceivable what an enchantment the scene itself lends to those delineations, from which its own most touching charm arises. But I will give you an abstract of our voyage, which lasted eight days, and if you have a map of Switzerland, you can follow me.

We left Montalegre at half past two on the 23d of June. The lake was calm, and after three hours of rowing we arrived at Hermance, a beautiful little village, containing a ruined tower, built, the villagers say, by Julius Cæsar. There were three other towers similar to it, which the Genevese destroyed for their own fortifications in 1560. We got into the tower by a kind of window. The walls are immensely solid, and the stone of which it is built so hard, that it yet retained the mark of chisels. The boatmen said, that this tower was once three times higher than it is now. There are two staircases in the thickness of the walls, one of which is entirely demolished, and the other half ruined, and only accessible by a ladder. The town itself, now an inconsiderable village inhabited by a few fishermen, was built by a Queen of Burgundy, and reduced to its present state by the inhabitants of Berne, who burnt and ravaged every thing they could find.

Leaving Hermance, we arrived at sunset at the village of Nerni. After looking at our lodgings, which were gloomy and dirty, we walked out by the side of the lake. It was beautiful to see the vast expanse of these purple and misty waters broken by the craggy islets near to its slant and "beached margin." There were many fish sporting in the lake, and multitudes were collected close to the rocks to catch the flies which inhabited them.

On returning to the village, we sat on a wall beside the lake, looking at some children who were playing at a game like ninepins. The children here appeared in an extraordinary way deformed and diseased. Most of them were crooked, and with enlarged throats; but one little boy had such exquisite grace in his mien and motions, as I never before saw equalled in a child. His countenance was beautiful for the expression with which it overflowed. There was a mixture of pride and gentleness in his eyes and lips, the indications of sensibility, which his education will probably pervert to misery or seduce to crime; but there was more of gentleness than of pride, and it seemed that the pride was tamed from its original wildness by the habitual exercise of milder feelings. My companion gave him a piece of money, which he took without speaking, with a sweet smile of easy thankfulness, and then with an unembarrassed air turned to his play. All this might scarcely be; but the imagination surely could not forbear to breathe into the most inanimate forms some likeness of its own visions, on such a serene and glowing evening, in this remote and romantic village, beside the calm lake that bore us hither.

On returning to our inn, we found that the servant had arranged our rooms, and deprived them of the greater portion of their former disconsolate appearance. They reminded my companion of Greece: it was five years, he said, since he had slept in such beds. The influence of the recollections excited by this circumstance on our conversation gradually faded, and I retired to rest with no unpleasant sensations, thinking of our journey tomorrow, and of the pleasure of recounting the little adventures of it when we return.

The next morning we passed Yvoire, a scattered village with an ancient castle, whose houses are interspersed with trees, and which stands at a little distance from Nerni, on the promontory which bounds a deep bay, some miles in extent. So soon as we arrived at this promontory, the lake began to assume an aspect of wilder magnificence. The mountains of Savoy, whose summits were bright with snow, descended in broken slopes to the lake: on high, the rocks were dark with pine forests, which become deeper and more immense, until the ice and snow mingle with the points of naked rock that pierce the blue air; but below, groves of walnut, chesnut, and oak, with openings of lawny fields, attested the milder climate.

As soon as we had passed the opposite promontory, we saw the river Drance, which descends from between a chasm in the mountains, and makes a plain near the lake, intersected by its divided streams. Thousands of *besolets*, beautiful water-birds, like sea-gulls, but smaller, with purple on their backs, take their station on the shallows, where its waters mingle with the lake. As we approached Evian, the mountains descended more precipitously to the lake, and masses of intermingled wood and rock overhung its shining spire.

We arrived at this town about seven o'clock, after a day which involved more rapid changes of atmosphere than I ever recollect to have observed before. The morning was cold and wet; then an easterly wind, and the clouds hard and high; then thunder showers, and wind shifting to every quarter; then a warm blast from the south, and summer clouds hanging over the peaks, with bright blue sky between. About half an hour after we had arrived at Evian, a few flashes of lightning came from a dark cloud, directly over head, and continued after the cloud had dispersed. "Diespiter, per pura tonantes egit equos:" a phenomenon which certainly had no influence on me, corresponding with that which it produced on Horace.

The appearance of the inhabitants of Evian is more wretched, diseased and poor, than I ever recollect to have seen. The contrast indeed between the subjects of the King of Sardinia and the citizens of the independent republics of Switzerland, affords a powerful illustration of the blighting mischiefs of despotism, within the space of a few miles. They have mineral waters here, *eaux savonneuses*, they call them. In the evening we had some difficulty about our passports, but so soon as the syndic heard my companion's rank and name, he apologized for the circumstance. The inn was good. During our voyage, on the distant height of a hill, covered [117] with pine-forests, we saw a ruined castle, which reminded me of those on the Rhine.

We left Evian on the following morning, with a wind of such violence as to permit but one sail to be carried. The waves also were exceedingly high, and our boat so heavily laden, that there appeared to be some danger. We arrived however safe at Mellerie, after passing with great speed mighty forests which overhung the lake, and lawns of exquisite verdure, and mountains with bare and icy points, which rose immediately from the summit of the rocks, whose bases were echoing to the waves.

We here heard that the Empress Maria Louisa had slept at Mellerie, [118] before the present inn was built, and when the accommodations were those of the most wretched village, in remembrance of St. Preux. How beautiful it is to find that the common sentiments of human nature can attach themselves to those who are the most removed from its duties and its enjoyments, when Genius pleads for their admission at the gate of Power. To own them was becoming in the Empress, and confirms the affectionate praise contained in the regret of a great and enlightened nation. A Bourbon dared not even to have remembered Rousseau. She owed this power to that democracy which her husband's dynasty outraged, and of which it was [119] however in some sort the representative among the nations of the earth. This little incident shews at once how unfit and how impossible it is for the ancient system of opinions, or for any power built upon a conspiracy to revive them, permanently to subsist among mankind. We dined there, and had some honey, the best I have ever tasted, the very essence of the mountain flowers, and as fragrant. Probably the village derives its name from this production. Mellerie is the well known scene of St. Preux's visionary exile; but Mellerie is indeed inchanted ground, were Rousseau no magician. Groves of pine, chesnut, and walnut overshadow it; magnificent and unbounded forests to [120] which England affords no parallel. In the midst of these woods are dells of lawny expanse, inconceivably verdant, adorned with a thousand of the rarest flowers and odorous with thyme.

The lake appeared somewhat calmer as we left Mellerie, sailing close to the banks, whose magnificence augmented with the turn of every promontory. But we congratulated ourselves too soon: the wind gradually increased in violence, until it blew tremendously; and as it came from the remotest extremity of the lake, produced waves of a frightful height, and covered the whole surface with a chaos of foam. One of our boatmen, who was a dreadfully stupid fellow, persisted in holding the sail at a time when the boat was on the point of being driven under water by the hurricane. On discovering his error, he let it entirely go, and the boat for a moment refused to obey the helm; in addition, the rudder was so broken as to render the management of it very difficult; one wave fell in, and then another. My companion, an excellent swimmer, took off his coat, I did the same, and we sat with our arms crossed, every instant expecting to be swamped. The sail was however again held, the boat obeyed the helm, and still in imminent peril from the immensity of the waves, we arrived in a few minutes at a sheltered port, in the village of St. Gingoux.

I felt in this near prospect of death a mixture of sensations, among which terror entered, though but subordinately. My feelings would have been less painful had I been alone; but I know that my companion would have attempted to save me, and I was overcome with humiliation, when I thought that his life might have been risked to preserve mine. When we arrived at St. Gingoux, the inhabitants, who stood on the shore, unaccustomed to see a vessel as frail as ours, and fearing to venture at all on such a sea, exchanged looks of wonder and congratulation with our boatmen, who, as well as ourselves, were well pleased to set foot on shore.

St. Gingoux is even more beautiful than Mellerie; the mountains are higher, and their loftiest points of elevation descend more abruptly to the lake. On high, the aerial summits still cherish great depths of snow in their ravines, and in the paths of their unseen torrents. One of the highest of these is called Roche de St. Julien, beneath whose pinnacles the forests become deeper and more extensive; the chesnut gives a peculiarity to the scene, which is most beautiful, and will make a picture in my memory, distinct from all other mountain scenes which I have ever before visited.

As we arrived here early, we took a *voiture* to visit the mouth of the Rhone. We went between the mountains and the lake, under groves of mighty chesnut trees, beside perpetual streams, which are nourished by the snows above, and form stalactites on the rocks, over which they fall. We saw an immense chesnut tree, which had been overthrown by the hurricane of the morning. The place where the Rhone joins the lake was marked by a line of tremendous breakers; the river is as rapid as when it leaves the lake, but is muddy and dark. We went about a league farther on the road to La Valais, and stopped at a castle called La Tour de Bouverie, which seems to be the frontier of Switzerland and Savoy, as we were asked for our passports, on the supposition of our proceeding to Italy.

On one side of the road was the immense Roche de St. Julien, which overhung it; through the gateway of the castle we saw the snowy mountains of La Valais, clothed in clouds, and on the other side was the willowy plain of the Rhone, in a character of striking contrast with the rest of the scene, bounded by the dark mountains that overhang Clarens, Vevai, and the lake that rolls between. In the midst of the plain rises a little isolated hill, on which the white spire of a church peeps from among the tufted chesnut woods. We returned to St. Gingoux before sunset, and I passed the evening in reading Julie.

As my companion rises late, I had time before breakfast, on the ensuing morning, to hunt the waterfalls of the river that fall into the lake at St. Gingoux. The stream is indeed, from the declivity over which it falls, only a succession of waterfalls, which roar over the rocks with a perpetual sound, and suspend their unceasing spray on the leaves and flowers that overhang and adorn its savage banks. The path that conducted along this river sometimes avoided the precipices of its shores, by leading through meadows; sometimes threaded the base of the perpendicular and caverned rocks. I gathered in these meadows a nosegay of such flowers as I never saw in England, and which I thought more beautiful for that rarity.

On my return, after breakfast, we sailed for Clarens, determining first to see the three mouths of the Rhone, and then the castle of Chillon; the day was fine, and the water calm. We passed from the blue waters of the lake over the stream of the Rhone, which is rapid even at a great distance from its confluence with the lake; the turbid waters mixed with those of the lake, but mixed with them unwillingly. (SEE NOUVELLE HELOISE, LETTRE 17, PART 4.) I read Julie all day; an overflowing, as it now seems, surrounded by the scenes which it has so wonderfully peopled, [128] of sublimest genius, and more than human sensibility. Mellerie, the Castle of Chillon, Clarens, the mountains of La Valais and Savoy, present themselves to the imagination as monuments of things that were once familiar, and of beings that were once dear to it. They were created indeed by one mind, but a mind so powerfully bright as to cast a shade of falsehood on the records that are called reality.

We passed on to the Castle of Chillon, and visited its dungeons and towers. These prisons are excavated below the lake; the principal dungeon is supported by seven columns, whose branching capitals support the roof. Close to the very walls, the lake is 800 [129] feet deep; iron rings are fastened to these columns, and on them were engraven a multitude of names, partly those of visitors, and partly doubtless of the prisoners, of whom now no memory remains, and who thus beguiled a solitude which they have long ceased to feel. One date was as ancient as 1670. At the commencement of the Reformation, and indeed long after that period, this dungeon was the receptacle of those who shook, or who denied the system of idolatry, from the effects of which mankind is even now slowly emerging.

Close to this long and lofty dungeon was a narrow cell, and beyond it one larger and far more lofty and dark, supported [130] upon two unornamented arches. Across one of these arches was a beam, now black and rotten, on which prisoners were hung in secret. I never saw a monument more terrible of that cold and inhuman tyranny, which it has been the delight of man to exercise over man. It was indeed one of those many tremendous fulfilments which render the "pernicies humani generis" of the great Tacitus, so solemn and irrefragable a prophecy. The gendarme, who conducted us over this castle, told us that there was an opening to the lake, by means of a secret spring, connected with which the whole dungeon might be filled with water before the prisoners could possibly escape!

[131] We proceeded with a contrary wind to Clarens, against a heavy swell. I never felt more strongly than on landing at Clarens, that the spirit of old times had deserted its once cherished habitation. A thousand times, thought I, have Julia and St. Preux walked on this terraced road, looking towards these mountains which I now behold; nay, treading on the ground where I now tread. From the window of our lodging our landlady pointed out "le bosquet de Julie." At least the inhabitants of this village are impressed with an idea, that the persons of that

romance had actual existence. In the evening we walked thither. It is indeed Julia's wood. The hay was making [132] under the trees; the trees themselves were aged, but vigorous, and interspersed with younger ones, which are destined to be their successors, and in future years, when we are dead, to afford a shade to future worshippers of nature, who love the memory of that tenderness and peace of which this was the imaginary abode. We walked forward among the vineyards, whose narrow terraces overlook this affecting scene. Why did the cold maxims of the world compel me at this moment to repress the tears of melancholy transport which it would have been so sweet to indulge, immeasurably, even until the darkness of night had swallowed up the objects which excited them?

[133] I forgot to remark, what indeed my companion remarked to me, that our danger from the storm took place precisely in the spot where Julie and her lover were nearly overset, and where St. Preux was tempted to plunge with her into the lake.

On the following day we went to see the castle of Clarens, a square strong house, with very few windows, surrounded by a double terrace that overlooks the valley, or rather the plain of Clarens. The road which conducted to it wound up the steep ascent through woods of walnut and chesnut. We gathered roses on the terrace, in the feeling that they might be the posterity of some planted by Julia's hand. We [134] sent their dead and withered leaves to the absent.

We went again to "the bosquet de Julie," and found that the precise spot was now utterly obliterated, and a heap of stones marked the place where the little chapel had once stood. Whilst we were execrating the author of this brutal folly, our guide informed us that the land belonged to the convent of St. Bernard, and that this outrage had been committed by their orders. I knew before, that if avarice could harden the hearts of men, a system of prescriptive religion has an influence far more inimical to natural sensibility. I know that an isolated man is sometimes restrained by shame from outraging the [135] venerable feelings arising out of the memory of genius, which once made nature even lovelier than itself; but associated man holds it as the very sacrament of his union to forswear all delicacy, all benevolence, all remorse, all that is true, or tender, or sublime.

We sailed from Clarens to Vevai. Vevai is a town more beautiful in its simplicity than any I have ever seen. Its market-place, a spacious square interspersed with trees, looks directly upon the mountains of Savoy and La Valais, the lake, and the valley of the Rhone. It was at Vevai that Rousseau conceived the design of Julie.

From Vevai we came to Ouchy, a village near Lausanne. The coasts of 136 the Pays de Vaud, though full of villages and vineyards, present an aspect of tranquillity and peculiar beauty which well compensates for the solitude which I am accustomed to admire. The hills are very high and rocky, crowned and interspersed with woods. Water-falls echo from the cliffs, and shine afar. In one place we saw the traces of two rocks of immense size, which had fallen from the mountain behind. One of these lodged in a room where a young woman was sleeping, without injuring her. The vineyards were utterly destroyed in its path, and the earth torn up.

The rain detained us two days at Ouchy. We however visited Lausanne, 137 and saw Gibbon's house. We were shewn the decayed summer-house where he finished his History, and the old acacias on the terrace, from which he saw Mont Blanc, after having written the last sentence. There is something grand and even touching in the regret which he expresses at the completion of his task. It was conceived amid the ruins of the Capitol. The sudden departure of his cherished and accustomed toil must have left him, like the death of a dear friend, sad and solitary.

My companion gathered some acacia leaves to preserve in remembrance of him. I refrained from doing so, fearing to outrage the greater and more 138 sacred name of Rousseau; the contemplation of whose imperishable creations had left no vacancy in my heart for mortal things. Gibbon had a cold and unimpassioned spirit. I never felt more inclination to rail at the prejudices which cling to such a thing, than now that Julie and Clarens, Lausanne and the Roman Empire, compelled me to a contrast between Rousseau and Gibbon.

When we returned, in the only interval of sunshine during the day, I walked on the pier which the lake was lashing with its waves. A rainbow spanned the lake, or rather rested one extremity of its arch upon the water, and the other at the foot of the mountains 139 of Savoy. Some white houses, I know not if they were those of Mellerie, shone through the yellow fire.

On Saturday the 30th of June we quitted Ouchy, and after two days of pleasant sailing arrived on Sunday evening at Montalegre.

S.

LETTER IV.

To T. P. Esq.

ST. MARTIN—SERVOZ—CHAMOUNI—MONTANVERT—MONT BLANC.

Hôtel de Londres, Chamouni,
July 22d, 1816.

Whilst you, my friend, are engaged in securing a home for us, we are wandering in search of recollections to embellish it. I do not err in conceiving that you are interested in details of all that is majestic or beautiful in nature; but how shall I describe to you the scenes by which I am now surrounded? To exhaust the epithets which express the astonishment and the admiration—the very excess of satisfied astonishment, where expectation scarcely acknowledged any boundary, is this, to impress upon your mind the images which fill mine now even till it overflow? I too have read the raptures of travellers; I will be warned by their example; I will simply detail to you all that I can relate, or all that, if related, would enable you to conceive of what we have done or seen since the morning of the 20th, when we left Geneva.

We commenced our intended journey to Chamouni at half-past eight in the morning. We passed through the champain country, which extends from Mont Salève to the base of the higher Alps. The country is sufficiently fertile, covered with corn fields and orchards, and intersected by sudden acclivities with flat summits. The day was cloudless and excessively hot, the Alps were perpetually in sight, and as we advanced, the mountains, which form their outskirts, closed in around us. We passed a bridge over a stream, which discharges itself into the Arve. The Arve itself, much swollen by the rains, flows constantly to the right of the road.

As we approached Bonneville through an avenue composed of a beautiful species of drooping poplar, we observed that the corn fields on each side were covered with inundation. Bonneville is a neat little town, with no conspicuous peculiarity, except the white towers of the prison, an extensive building overlooking the town. At Bonneville the Alps commence, one of which, clothed by forests, rises almost immediately from the opposite bank of the Arve.

From Bonneville to Cluses the road conducts through a spacious and fertile plain, surrounded on all sides by mountains, covered like those of Mellerie with forests of intermingled pine and chesnut. At Cluses the road turns suddenly to the right, following the Arve along the chasm, which it seems to have hollowed for itself among the 144 perpendicular mountains. The scene assumes here a more savage and colossal character; the valley becomes narrow, affording no more space than is sufficient for the river and the road. The pines descend to the banks, imitating with their irregular spires, the pyramidal crags which lift themselves far above the regions of forest into the deep azure of the sky, and among the white dazzling clouds. The scene, at the distance of half a mile from Cluses, differs from that of Matlock in little else than in the immensity of its proportions, and in its untameable, inaccessible solitude, inhabited only by the goats which we saw browsing on the rocks.

145 Near Maglans, within a league of each other, we saw two waterfalls. They were no more than mountain rivulets, but the height from which they fell, at least of TWELVE hundred feet, made them assume a character inconsistent with the smallness of their stream. The first fell from the overhanging brow of a black precipice on an enormous rock, precisely resembling some colossal Egyptian statue of a female deity. It struck the head of the visionary image, and gracefully dividing there, fell from it in folds of foam more like to cloud than water, imitating a veil of the most exquisite woof. It then united, concealing the lower part of the statue, and hiding itself in 146 a winding of its channel, burst into a deeper fall, and crossed our route in its path towards the Arve.

The other waterfall was more continuous and larger. The violence with which it fell made it look more like some shape which an exhalation had assumed, than like water, for it streamed beyond the mountain, which appeared dark behind it, as it might have appeared behind an evanescent cloud.

The character of the scenery continued the same until we arrived at St. Martin (called in the maps Sallanches) the mountains perpetually becoming more elevated, exhibiting at every turn of the road more craggy summits, loftier and wider extent of forests, darker and more deep recesses.

147 The following morning we proceeded from St. Martin on mules to Chamouni, accompanied by two guides. We proceeded, as we had done the preceding day, along the valley of the Arve, a

valley surrounded on all sides by immense mountains, whose rugged precipices are intermixed on high with dazzling snow. Their bases were still covered with the eternal forests, which perpetually grew darker and more profound as we approached the inner regions of the mountains.

On arriving at a small village, at the distance of a league from St. Martin, we dismounted from our mules, and were conducted by our guides to view a cascade. We beheld an immense body of water fall two hundred and fifty feet, dashing from rock to rock, and casting a spray which formed a mist around it, in the midst of which hung a multitude of sunbows, which faded or became unspeakably vivid, as the inconstant sun shone through the clouds. When we approached near to it, the rain of the spray reached us, and our clothes were wetted by the quick-falling but minute particles of water. The cataract fell from above into a deep craggy chasm at our feet, where, changing its character to that of a mountain stream, it pursued its course towards the Arve, roaring over the rocks that impeded its progress.

As we proceeded, our route still lay through the valley, or rather, as it had now become, the vast ravine, which is at once the couch and the creation of the terrible Arve. We ascended, winding between mountains whose immensity staggers the imagination. We crossed the path of a torrent, which three days since had descended from the thawing snow, and torn the road away.

We dined at Servoz, a little village, where there are lead and copper mines, and where we saw a cabinet of natural curiosities, like those of Keswick and Bethgelert. We saw in this cabinet some chamois' horns, and the horns of an exceedingly rare animal called the bouquetin, which inhabits the desarts of snow to the south of Mont Blanc: it is an animal of the stag kind; its horns weigh at least twenty-seven English pounds. It is inconceivable how so small an animal could support so inordinate a weight. The horns are of a very peculiar conformation, being broad, massy, and pointed at the ends, and surrounded with a number of rings, which are supposed to afford an indication of its age: there were seventeen rings on the largest of these horns.

From Servoz three leagues remain to Chamouni.—Mont Blanc was before us—the Alps, with their innumerable glaciers on high all around, closing in the complicated windings of the single vale—forests inexpressibly beautiful, but majestic in their beauty—intermingled beech and pine, and oak, overshadowed our road, or receded, whilst lawns of such verdure as I have never seen before occupied these openings, and gradually became darker in their recesses. Mont Blanc was before us, but it was covered with cloud; its base, furrowed with dreadful gaps, was seen above. Pinnacles of snow intolerably bright, part of the chain connected with Mont Blanc, shone through the clouds at intervals on high. I never knew—I never imagined what mountains were before. The immensity of these aerial summits excited, when they suddenly burst upon the sight, a sentiment of extatic wonder, not unallied to madness. And remember this was all one scene, it all pressed home to our regard and our imagination. Though it embraced a vast extent of space, the snowy pyramids which shot into the bright blue sky seemed to overhang our path; the ravine, clothed with gigantic pines, and black with its depth below, so deep that the very roaring of the untameable Arve, which rolled through it, could not be heard above—all was as much our own, as if we had been the creators of such impressions in the minds of others as now occupied our own. Nature was the poet, whose harmony held our spirits more breathless than that of the divinest.

As we entered the valley of Chamouni (which in fact may be considered as a continuation of those which we have followed from Bonneville and Cluses) clouds hung upon the mountains at the distance perhaps of 6000 feet from the earth, but so as effectually to conceal not only Mont Blanc, but the other AIGUILLES, as they call them here, attached and subordinate to it. We were travelling along the valley, when suddenly we heard a sound as of the burst of smothered thunder rolling above; yet there was something earthly in the sound, that told us it could not be thunder. Our guide hastily pointed out to us a part of the mountain opposite, from whence the sound came. It was an avalanche. We saw the smoke of its path among the rocks, and continued to hear at intervals the bursting of its fall. It fell on the bed of a torrent, which it displaced, and presently we saw its tawny-coloured waters also spread themselves over the ravine, which was their couch.

We did not, as we intended, visit the GLACIER DE BOISSON to-day, although it descends within a few minutes' walk of the road, wishing to survey it at least when unfatigued. We saw this glacier which comes close to the fertile plain, as we passed, its surface was broken into a thousand unaccountable figures: conical and pyramidical crystallizations, more than fifty feet in height, rise from its surface, and precipices of ice, of dazzling splendour, overhang the woods and meadows of the vale. This glacier winds upwards from the valley, until it joins the masses of frost from which it was produced above, winding through its own ravine like a bright belt flung over the black region of pines. There is more in all these scenes than mere magnitude of proportion: there is a majesty of outline; there is an awful grace in the very colours which invest these wonderful shapes—a charm which is peculiar to them, quite distinct even from the reality of their unutterable greatness.

July 24.

Yesterday morning we went to the source of the Arveiron. It is about a league from this village; the river rolls forth impetuously from an arch of ice, and spreads itself in many streams over a vast space of the valley, ravaged and laid bare by its inundations. The glacier by which its waters are nourished, overhangs this cavern and the plain, and the forests of pine which surround it, with terrible precipices of solid ice. On the other side rises the immense glacier of Montanvert, fifty miles in extent, occupying a chasm among mountains of inconceivable height, and of forms so pointed and abrupt, that they seem to pierce the sky. From this glacier we saw as we sat on a rock, close to one of the streams of the Arveiron, masses of ice detach themselves from on high, and rush with a loud dull noise into the vale. The violence of their fall turned them into powder, which flowed over the rocks in imitation of waterfalls, whose ravines they usurped and filled.

In the evening I went with Ducrée, my guide, the only tolerable person I have seen in this country, to visit the glacier of Boisson. This glacier, like that of Montanvert, comes close to the vale, overhanging the green meadows and the dark woods with the dazzling whiteness of its precipices and pinnacles, which are like spires of radiant crystal, covered with a net-work of frosted silver. These glaciers flow perpetually into the valley, ravaging in their slow but irresistible progress the pastures and the forests which surround them, performing a work of desolation in ages, which a river of lava might accomplish in an hour, but far more irretrievably; for where the ice has once descended, the hardiest plant refuses to grow; if even, as in some extraordinary instances, it should recede after its progress has once commenced. The glaciers perpetually move onward, at the rate of a foot each day, with a motion that commences at the spot where, on the boundaries of perpetual congelation, they are produced by the freezing of the waters which arise from the partial melting of the eternal snows. They drag with them from the regions whence they derive their origin, all the ruins of the mountain, enormous rocks, and immense accumulations of sand and stones. These are driven onwards by the irresistible stream of solid ice; and when they arrive at a declivity of the mountain, sufficiently rapid, roll down, scattering ruin. I saw one of these rocks which had descended in the spring, (winter here is the season of silence and safety) which measured forty feet in every direction.

The verge of a glacier, like that of Boisson, presents the most vivid image of desolation that it is possible to conceive. No one dares to approach it; for the enormous pinnacles of ice which perpetually fall, are perpetually reproduced. The pines of the forest, which bound it at one extremity, are overthrown and shattered to a wide extent at its base. There is something inexpressibly dreadful in the aspect of the few branchless trunks, which, nearest to the ice rifts, still stand in the uprooted soil. The meadows perish, overwhelmed with sand and stones. Within this last year, these glaciers have advanced three hundred feet into the valley. Saussure, the naturalist, says, that they have their periods of increase and decay: the people of the country hold an opinion entirely different; but as I judge, more probable. It is agreed by all, that the snow on the summit of Mont Blanc and the neighbouring mountains perpetually augments, and that ice, in the form of glaciers, subsists without melting in the valley of Chamouni during its transient and variable summer. If the snow which produces this glacier must augment, and the heat of the valley is no obstacle to the perpetual existence of such masses of ice as have already descended into it, the consequence is obvious; the glaciers must augment and will subsist, at least until they have overflowed this vale.

I will not pursue Buffon's sublime but gloomy theory—that this globe which we inhabit will at some future period be changed into a mass of frost by the encroachments of the polar ice, and of that produced on the most elevated points of the earth. Do you, who assert the supremacy of Ahriman, imagine him throned among these desolating snows, among these palaces of death and frost, so sculptured in this their terrible magnificence by the adamantine hand of necessity, and that he casts around him, as the first essays of his final usurpation, avalanches, torrents, rocks, and thunders, and above all these deadly glaciers, at once the proof and symbols of his reign;—add to this, the degradation of the human species—who in these regions are half deformed or idiotic, and most of whom are deprived of any thing that can excite interest or admiration. This is a part of the subject more mournful and less sublime; but such as neither the poet nor the philosopher should disdain to regard.

This morning we departed, on the promise of a fine day, to visit the glacier of Montanvert. In that part where it fills a slanting valley, it is called the Sea of Ice. This valley is 950 toises, or 7600 feet above the level of the sea. We had not proceeded far before the rain began to fall, but we persisted until we had accomplished more than half of our journey, when we returned, wet through.

Chamouni, July 25th.

We have returned from visiting the glacier of Montanvert, or as it is called, the Sea of Ice, a scene in truth of dizzying wonder. The path that winds to it along the side of a mountain, now clothed with pines, now intersected with snowy hollows, is wide and steep. The cabin of Montanvert is three leagues from Chamouni, half of which distance is performed on mules, not so sure footed, but that on the first day the one which I rode fell in what the guides call a *mauvais pas*, so that I narrowly escaped being precipitated down the mountain. We passed over a hollow covered with snow, down which vast stones are accustomed to roll. One had fallen the preceding day, a little time after we had returned: our guides desired us to pass quickly, for it is said that sometimes the least sound will accelerate their descent. We arrived at Montanvert, however, safe.

On all sides precipitous mountains, the abodes of unrelenting frost, surround this vale: their sides are banked up with ice and snow, broken, heaped high, and exhibiting terrific chasms. The summits are sharp and naked pinnacles, whose overhanging steepness will not even permit snow to rest upon them. Lines of dazzling ice occupy here and there their perpendicular rifts, and shine through the driving vapours with inexpressible brilliance: they pierce the clouds like things not belonging to this earth. The vale itself is filled with a mass of undulating ice, and has an ascent sufficiently gradual even to the remotest abysses of these horrible desarts. It is only half a league (about two miles) in breadth, and seems much less. It exhibits an appearance as if frost had suddenly bound up the waves and whirlpools of a mighty torrent. We walked some distance upon its surface. The waves are elevated about 12 or 15 feet from the surface of the mass, which is intersected by long gaps of unfathomable depth, the ice of whose sides is more beautifully azure than the sky. In these regions every thing changes, and is in motion. This vast mass of ice has one general progress, which ceases neither day nor night; it breaks and bursts for ever: some undulations sink while others rise; it is never the same. The echo of rocks, or of the ice and snow which fall from their overhanging precipices, or roll from their aerial summits, scarcely ceases for one moment. One would think that Mont Blanc, like the god of the Stoics, was a vast animal, and that the frozen blood for ever circulated through his stony veins.

We dined (M***, C***, and I) on the grass, in the open air, surrounded by this scene. The air is piercing and clear. We returned down the mountain, sometimes encompassed by the driving vapours, sometimes cheered by the sunbeams, and arrived at our inn by seven o'clock.

Montalegre, July 28th.

The next morning we returned through the rain to St. Martin. The scenery had lost something of its immensity, thick clouds hanging over the highest mountains; but visitings of sunset intervened between the showers, and the blue sky shone between the accumulated clouds of snowy whiteness which brought them; the dazzling mountains sometimes glittered through a chasm of the clouds above our heads, and all the charm of its grandeur remained. We repassed *Pont Pellisier*, a wooden bridge over the Arve, and the ravine of the Arve. We repassed the pine forests which overhang the defile, the chateau of St. Michel, a haunted ruin, built on the edge of a precipice, and shadowed over by the eternal forest. We repassed the vale of Servoz, a vale more beautiful, because more luxuriant, than that of Chamouni. Mont Blanc forms one of the sides of this vale also, and the other is inclosed by an irregular amphitheatre of enormous mountains, one of which is in ruins, and fell fifty years ago into the higher part of the valley: the smoke of its fall was seen in Piedmont, and people went from Turin to investigate whether a volcano had not burst forth among the Alps. It continued falling many days, spreading, with the shock and thunder of its ruin, consternation into the neighbouring vales. In the evening we arrived at St. Martin. The next day we wound through the valley, which I have described before, and arrived in the evening at our home.

We have bought some specimens of minerals and plants, and two or three crystal seals, at Mont Blanc, to preserve the remembrance of having approached it. There is a cabinet of *Histoire Naturelle* at Chamouni, just as at Keswick, Matlock, and Clifton; the proprietor of which is the very vilest specimen of that vile species of quack that, together with the whole army of aubergistes and guides, and indeed the entire mass of the population, subsist on the weakness and credulity of travellers as leaches subsist on the sick. The most interesting of my purchases is a large collection of all the seeds of rare alpine plants, with their names written upon the outside of the papers that contain them. These I mean to colonize in my garden in England, and to permit you to make what choice you please from them. They are companions which the Celandine—the classic Celandine, need not despise; they are as wild and more daring than he, and will tell him tales of things even as touching and sublime as the gaze of a vernal poet.

Did I tell you that there are troops of wolves among these mountains? In the winter they descend into the vallies, which the snow occupies six months of the year, and devour every thing that they can find out of doors. A wolf is more powerful than the fiercest and strongest dog. There are no bears in these regions. We heard, when we were at Lucerne, that they were occasionally found in the forests which surround that lake. Adieu.

S.

LINES

WRITTEN IN THE VALE OF CHAMOUNI.

MONT BLANC.

LINES WRITTEN IN THE VALE OF CHAMOUNI.

I.
The everlasting universe of things
Flows through the mind, and rolls its rapid waves,
Now dark—now glittering—now reflecting gloom—
Now lending splendour, where from secret springs
The source of human thought its tribute brings
Of waters,—with a sound but half its own,

Such as a feeble brook will oft assume
In the wild woods, among the mountains lone,
Where waterfalls around it leap for ever,
Where woods and winds contend, and a vast river
Over its rocks ceaselessly bursts and raves.

II.

Thus thou, Ravine of Arve—dark, deep Ravine—
Thou many-coloured, many-voiced vale,
Over whose pines, and crags, and caverns sail
Fast cloud shadows and sunbeams: awful scene,
Where Power in likeness of the Arve comes down
From the ice gulphs that gird his secret throne,
Bursting through these dark mountains like the flame
Of lightning thro' the tempest;—thou dost lie,
Thy giant brood of pines around thee clinging,
Children of elder time, in whose devotion
The chainless winds still come and ever came
To drink their odours, and their mighty swinging
To hear—an old and solemn harmony;
Thine earthly rainbows stretched across the sweep
Of the ethereal waterfall, whose veil
Robes some unsculptured image; the strange sleep
Which when the voices of the desert fail
Wraps all in its own deep eternity;—
Thy caverns echoing to the Arve's commotion,
A loud, lone sound no other sound can tame;
Thou art pervaded with that ceaseless motion,
Thou art the path of that unresting sound—
Dizzy Ravine! and when I gaze on thee
I seem as in a trance sublime and strange
To muse on my own separate phantasy,
My own, my human mind, which passively
Now renders and receives fast influencings,
Holding an unremitting interchange
With the clear universe of things around;
One legion of wild thoughts, whose wandering wings
Now float above thy darkness, and now rest
Where that or thou art no unbidden guest,
In the still cave of the witch Poesy,
Seeking among the shadows that pass by
Ghosts of all things that are, some shade of thee,
Some phantom, some faint image; till the breast
From which they fled recalls them, thou art there!

III.
Some say that gleams of a remoter world
Visit the soul in sleep,—that death is slumber,
And that its shapes the busy thoughts outnumber
Of those who wake and live.—I look on high;
Has some unknown omnipotence unfurled
The veil of life and death? or do I lie
In dream, and does the mightier world of sleep
Spread far around and inaccessibly
Its circles? For the very spirit fails,
Driven like a homeless cloud from steep to steep
That vanishes among the viewless gales!
Far, far above, piercing the infinite sky,
Mont Blanc appears,—still, snowy, and serene—
Its subject mountains their unearthly forms
Pile around it, ice and rock; broad vales between
Of frozen floods, unfathomable deeps,
Blue as the overhanging heaven, that spread
And wind among the accumulated steeps;
A desert peopled by the storms alone,
Save when the eagle brings some hunter's bone,
And the wolf tracts her there—how hideously
Its shapes are heaped around! rude, bare, and high,
Ghastly, and scarred, and riven.—Is this the scene
Where the old Earthquake-dæmon taught her young
Ruin? Were these their toys? or did a sea
Of fire, envelope once this silent snow?
None can reply—all seems eternal now.
The wilderness has a mysterious tongue
Which teaches awful doubt, or faith so mild,
So solemn, so serene, that man may be
But for such faith with nature reconciled;
Thou hast a voice, great Mountain, to repeal
Large codes of fraud and woe; not understood
By all, but which the wise, and great, and good
Interpret, or make felt, or deeply feel.
IV.
The fields, the lakes, the forests, and the streams,
Ocean, and all the living things that dwell
Within the dædal earth; lightning, and rain,
Earthquake, and fiery flood, and hurricane,
The torpor of the year when feeble dreams
Visit the hidden buds, or dreamless sleep

Holds every future leaf and flower;—the bound
With which from that detested trance they leap;
The works and ways of man, their death and birth,
And that of him and all that his may be;
All things that move and breathe with toil and sound
Are born and die; revolve, subside and swell.
Power dwells apart in its tranquillity
Remote, serene, and inaccessible:
And THIS, the naked countenance of earth,
On which I gaze, even these primæval mountains
Teach the adverting mind. The glaciers creep
Like snakes that watch their prey, from their far fountains,
Slow rolling on; there, many a precipice,
Frost and the Sun in scorn of mortal power
Have piled: dome, pyramid, and pinnacle,
A city of death, distinct with many a tower
And wall impregnable of beaming ice.
Yet not a city, but a flood of ruin
Is there, that from the boundaries of the sky
Rolls its perpetual stream; vast pines are strewing
Its destined path, or in the mangled soil
Branchless and shattered stand; the rocks, drawn down
From yon remotest waste, have overthrown
The limits of the dead and living world,
Never to be reclaimed. The dwelling-place
Of insects, beasts, and birds, becomes its spoil;
Their food and their retreat for ever gone,
So much of life and joy is lost. The race
Of man, flies far in dread; his work and dwelling
Vanish, like smoke before the tempest's stream,
And their place is not known. Below, vast caves
Shine in the rushing torrent's restless gleam,
Which from those secret chasms in tumult welling
Meet in the vale, and one majestic River,
The breath and blood of distant lands, for ever
Rolls its loud waters to the ocean waves.
Breathes its swift vapours to the circling air.
V.
Mont Blanc yet gleams on high:—the power is there,
The still and solemn power of many sights,
And many sounds, and much of life and death.
In the calm darkness of the moonless nights,
In the lone glare of day, the snows descend

Upon that Mountain; none beholds them there,
Nor when the flakes burn in the sinking sun,
Or the star-beams dart through them:—Winds contend
Silently there, and heap the snow with breath
Rapid and strong, but silently! Its home
The voiceless lightning in these solitudes
Keeps innocently, and like vapour broods
Over the snow. The secret strength of things
Which governs thought, and to the infinite dome
Of heaven is as a law, inhabits thee!
And what were thou, and earth, and stars, and sea,
If to the human mind's imaginings
Silence and solitude were vacancy?
June 23, 1816.
Reynell, Printer, 45, Broad-street,
Golden-square.

Printed in Great Britain
by Amazon